Copyright © 2022 Sylvia Hawkins Little, Ph.D.
All rights reserved. No part of this book
maybe reproduced, stored in a retrieval system, or
transmitted in any form or by any means, electronic, mechanical,
photocopying, recording, or otherwise without written
permission of the publisher, Epic Press, except
for the inclusion of brief quotations in
an acknowledge review.

Library of Congress Cataloging-in-Publication Data
LCCN: 2021930192
LITTLE, PH.D, SYLVIA HAWKINS

THANK A BLACK MAN: 1 IN A SERIES
LEWIS HOWARD LATIMER - ILLUMINATION

Summary: THANK A BLACK MAN: 1 IN A SERIES. LEWIS HOWARD LATIMER - ILLUMINATION is a (bio poem). Born in 1884 to runaway enslaven parents, had very little formal education, yet during his lifetime he obtained numerous patents; and was renown worldwide for his electrical lightning expertise. ISBN: 978-1-941185-02-5 (trade pbk); ISBN:9978-1-941185-03-2 (hbk); 978-1-941185-04-9 (ebk). 1 African American inventors—Biography—Science and Technology—Juvenile literature. 2. Inventors—United States—History—19th Century—Juvenile literature. 3. Inventors—United States—History—20th Century—Juvenile literature. 4. Stories in rhyme.

Printed In the United States of America
First Printing 2022

Graphic Designer
Dr. Sylvia Hawkins Little. PH.D.
Illustrator
Inventor Images: Mateo Tedin
Editors
Grant F. Little, III
Greer Hudson Little
Eleanor Renee Rodriguez, PH.D.

PUBLISHER
EPIC PRESS
P. O. BOX 141624
AUSTIN, TEXAS, 78714-1624
www.epic-press.com

Thank A Black Man: 1 In A Series

Lewis Howard Latimer - Illumination
Sylvia Hawkins Little, Ph.D.

A tribute to my
mother, daughter, and father,
Rita Johnson Hawkins Cave, Lisa Little
and Darnell H. Hawkins, Sr. who used their
time, talent and energies to make
a difference for others.

Honoring "Black Difference Makers"
Black men and women who through the years used their
ingenuity, time, and energies to make life better for everyone.
We now give credit to many who often did not receive
it at the time and sometimes still have not.
www.ThankABlackMan.com

Stroll down any street,
 "Tell me? What do you see?
Examples of Blacks' ingenuity
 that make life better for you and me.

Many things are quite different
from the way they used to be.
Things generally are taken for granted.
Things we do not often see.

Imagine how it was long ago
    on a dark and dreary night.
When candles, kerosene lanterns or gas
    lamps provided the only indoor light.

Lewis Howard Latimer
    made sure no one had to ponder.
An engineer, draftsman, legal expert,
    and inventor, he was a wonder.

The fourth child of George and Rebecca,
    Latimer was born on September 4, 1848.
His parents, enslaved runaways, had traveled
    north and settled in Boston, a safe place.

During their travels North, skin color
    determined the roles they had to play.
Light skin George was a plantation owner
    while dark skin Rebecca posed as his enslaved.

From his boyhood background,
   it was unlikely to predict fame.
Yet, when he died in 1928, thousands
   knew Lewis Howard Latimer's name.

Before ten, he went to school and after
> school he worked in his father's barbershop.

After ten, he worked full-time with his
> father hanging paper and school stopped.

Leaving school early to work with parents was
> typical for children in the 19th century.

Unlike the South, education was free for
> all in Massachusetts, but not compulsory.

A former employee
> of father's enslaver recognized him.

He was determined to take him
> back to Virginia where his future was grim.

The situation with his fathers'
> enslaver gained great notoriety.

It went up to the Massachusetts Supreme
> Court -- a trial that everyone wanted to see.

His father was quite lucky, he was defended
> by two abolitionists and activists of note.

Frederick Douglass and William Lloyd
> Garrison's success was one to connote.

George's community, former enslaved people
    and abolitionists, rallied against his arrest.
Raising funds to buy George's
    freedom, the solution all deemed the best.

Many believe the Dred Scott Decision
    caused George Latimer to later disappear.
Or his former enslaver
    caught him when he wasn't looking in his rear.

The Dred Scott Decision in 1857
    placed on many enslaved people an unfair weight.
Without papers an enslave person couldn't be
    considered a free man even if he lived in a free state.

Unable to support four children
    after her husband disappeared,
his brothers were sent to a farm school
    and his sister to friends to be reared.

Latimer stayed with his mother until
    she went to sea as a ship stewardess.
He went to join his brothers at the
    State Farm School because it was best.

Latimer hated manual labor (working in the fields, a farm school requirement. When his brother William offered a way out, he was happy to leave this confinement.

They traveled by night, slept during the day,
    and scrounged or stole food along the way
-walking, running, or stealing railroad rides,
    covering 80 miles to Boston, side by side.

Except for the Underground Railroad,
    their journey to Boston, one might say,
resembled the trips runaway slaves made
    to freedom in the North, in many ways.

Arriving back in Boston at thirteen, job
    opportunities were few and far between.
Latimer took many
    odd jobs about which he wasn't too keen.

Joining the United States Navy at fifteen,
    Latimer fought in the Civil War.
A cabin boy on the U.S. Massasoit
    gunboat, he honored the Union Star.

After the war, Latimer worked as an
    office assistant for a patent law corporation.
Protecting inventors' rights was
    Crosby, Halstead, and Gould's specialization.

While draftsmen typically acquired
    their skills from formal education.
This profession path wasn't available
    to Latimer for his chosen vocation.

An excellent reader and extremely
    skilled with drafting tools and pen,
Latimer emulated and surpassed
    the draftsmen sketches around him.

When his sketches of patent
    drawing caught his employers' attention,
Latimer was promoted to a junior draftsman
    and eventually to a head draftsman position.

Because of the U.S. Patent Office's strict requirements for illustrations, Latimer as head draftsmen played a key role in the preparation of patent applications.

In November 1873, his life would change when Mary Willson Lewis became his wife.

Later into this union two daughters were born to complete his family life.

In 1874 with Charles Brown, a co-worker,
  Latimer's patented his first invention.
Their train bathroom compartment
  improvement exceeded their intention.

In one special aspect,
  Lewis Latimer was quite unique.
He worked with both Alexander Graham
  Bell and Thomas Edison—quite a feat.

When Latimer worked with Alexander
   Graham Bell in 1876, time was tight.
To complete the patent application,
   Latimer worked all night.

Bell's telephone patent application
   was delivered with just hours to spare.
Submitted on Feb. 14, 1876,
   Bell's application beat a similar device there.

Latimer left Crosby, Halstead & Gould
   when the company's principals retired in 1876.
He held several jobs in
   the Boston area, but he never found a good fix.

Latimer moved to Bridgeport,

    Connecticut in 1879 to join his sister and other family.

Here he found work in a machine shop,

    as the only black man attracted attention — naturally.

There he met Hiram Stevens Maxim, a renowed

    inventor, who was exceedingly curious about him.

Maxim, the owner of the U.S. Electric

    Lightning Company, invited Latimer to join them.

Thus Latimer began

    the first stage of his "Illumination Destiny"

when he went to work for Hiram Stevens

    Maxim's at his U.S. Electric Lighting Company.

After he developed a new long lasting light
>   bulb filament, Latimer had a rapid "de facto"
graduation from draftsman to electrical
>   engineer and was made a key team member.

As assistant manager and chief engineer
>   for Hiram Maxium, Edison's competition,
Latimer enhanced his knowledge on
>   electrical light construction and operation.

Before long the electric light bulb's
>   short burn rate caught his attention.
Improvement became a necessity,
>   then it was a reality, finally his invention.

Lewis Howard Latimer did not
    invented the electric light bulb that is true.
However, there is one
    thing that is important point out to you.

Thomas Edison

    invented the electric light bulb that is true.

However, Latimer's 1882 patent, made the
    bulb's life span longer and lowered the price to you.

Latimer's 1882 manufacturing process for
    making new electric light bulbs last and shine
is still considered a critical technical achievement
    in the evolution of electric light in our time.

Edison's paper filament electric light bulb burned too fast. Latimer's carbon filament electric light bulb was designed to last.

*Antique Reproduction of carbon filament electric light bulb available today at https://www.lightbulbs.com/category/nostalgic-antique-light-bulbs

As the U. S. Light Company's Chief
    Electrical Engineer, Latimer was in great demand.
His abilities in electric
    lightning became well known throughout the land.

Eventually, as more
    major cities began wiring their streets for electricity,
Latimer was requested to
    lead their planning teams. He was the man to see.

Latimer traveled near and
    far, sharing his knowledge on electricity.
For lighting government
    buildings, railroad stations and cities.

Philadelphia, New York City and Montreal's
    first electric light plants were more than whims.
Like Canada, London and New England's major
    thoroughfare installation teams were lead by him.

\Moving to London with his wife, he established in one
    year a branch of Maxium's Incandescent Light Factory.
He taught all aspects of light
    bulb making and the art of blowing glass for all to see.

Latimer's 1984 departure from the U. S.
    Light Company put him in the middle of a rivarly.
Thomas Edison, Maxium's rival knew of his expertise
    but offered only a draftsman position with his company.

Supposdly hired for his drafting expertise,
    Latimer legal section placement was not on a whim.
Edison's company won
    many patent litigation court cases because of him.

Commissioned by Edison in 1890, the first engineering
    handbook on lighting systems was penned by him.
"Incandescent Electric Lighting: A Practical Description of
    the Edison System", became a standard reference; a gem.

When General Electric was formed by
    merging Edison's company with his rivals in 1892,
Edison again called on Latimore to
    protect his interest as this merger was going through.

In 1918, he became a charter member; the only African
America on Edison Pioneers, an elite research team.
Membership in this group represented the highest
honor to individuals in the electrical field's academe.

His remarkable legacy of inventions earned him
seven U. S. government patents - not all electricity.
They were wide and varied and
not all dealth with electricity -- go to page 33 to see.

Latimer was a flutist, artist, civil rights' activist, teacher,
consumate volunteer as well as a poet and playwright.
His published
poetry book is titled, "Poems of Love and Life".

When Latimer
    died on December 11, 1928, many would say,
his contributions
    made this world better in so many ways.

His remarkable legacy of inventions
    is documented by seven U. S. government patents.
They included his more famous lamp
    fixtures well as a less known book supporter patent.

Anyone with very little formal education who played a major
    role in the development of electricity is impressive.
And as a Black man born in the 19th century,
    his many successes made him even more impressive.

From his boyhood background,
    it was unlikely to predict fame.
Yet, when he died in 1928, thousands
    knew Lewis Howard Latimer's name.

Without a doubt—as you trace the progress of this great land, you'll have to take time to honor and thank "A Black Man."

"I was one of the first pioneers of the electric lighting industry from its creation until it had become worldwide in its influence".

~Lewis Howard Latimer~

One of the most important
    Black inventors of all time.
Latimer is renown because his abilities
    with lighting helped the world shine.

The magnitude of importance
    for his most famous discovery
must not be overlooked.
    It holds an important place in history.

He was a wonder—a son, brother, husband,
    father, engineer, legal expert, inventor, draftsman,
author, poet, teacher, musician and philanthropist
    —a self-taught man, A Renaissance Man.

LATIMER'S PATENTS

U.S. Patent Number	Description	Date
147,363	Water-Closets (toilets) for Railway Cars (with Charles W. Brown)	February 10, 1874
247,097	Electric Lamp (with Joseph V. Nicholas)	September 13, 1881
252,386	Process of Manufacturing Carbons	January 17, 1882
255,212	Globe Supporter for Electric Lamps (with John Tregoning)	March 21, 1882
334,078	Apparatus for Cooling and Disinfecting (Witnessed by Mary Latimer)	January 12, 1886
557,076	Locking Rack for Hats, Coats, and Umbrella	March 24, 1896
781,890	Book Supporter	February 2, 1905
968,787	Lamp fixture (with Charles W. Brown)	August 30, 1910

Sources:
http://edison.rutgers.edu/latimer/latpats.htm
http://www.ideafinder.com/history/inventors/latimer.htm

REFERENCES

Fouché, Rayvon, Black Inventors in the Age of Segregation. Baltimore & London: The John Hopkins University Press (2003)

Hayden, Robert C., 9 African American Inventors. Frederick, Maryland: Twenty-First Century Books, A Division of Henry Holt and Co., Inc. (1972)

Van Sertima, Ivan, Blacks in Science: Ancient and Modern. New Brunswick, New Jersey: Transition Books, 1984

http://african-americaninventors.org/

http://www.answers.com/topic/lewis-h-latimer

http://www.blackinventor.com/

http://www.eng.wayne.edu/news.php?id=2013

http://www.nps.gov/archive/edis/edisonia/graphics/10114016.jpg Founding members of Edison Pioneers at organizational meeting;1/24/18;{10.114/16}

http://teacher.scholastic.com/activities/bhistory/inventors/

GLOSSARY

Academe—the academic world.

Application—a written request; a way of being used; in computing, an application program.

Compulsory—must do, no choice, required. Education is compulsory up to certain age in all states.

Connote— to signify or suggest (certain meanings, ideas, etc.) in addition to the explicit or primary meaning: i.e. If a student is called a "scholar," it connotes that this person is serious, diligent, and intelligent.

Constitution— the basic beliefs and laws of a nation, state, or social group that establish the powers and duties of the government and guarantee certain rights to the people.

Construction—something built or put together, job or business of construction.

Consummate— extremely skilled and accomplished.

Contribution— to donate something, such as money, time, or talent, to a common fund or group effort.

Corporation—a group of people recognized by law and authorized to carry out certain functions with powers independent of the individual members.; any group of people who function as a unified whole.

Draftsman—a person who draws detailed plans and designs

Dred Scott Decision— The Supreme Court decision: --- Dred Scott v. Sandford was issued on March 6, 1857. Delivered by Chief Justice Roger Taney, this opinion declared that slaves were not citizens of the United States and could not sue in Federal courts. In addition, this decision declared that the Missouri Compromise was unconstitutional, and that Congress did not have the authority to prohibit slavery in the territories. The Dred Scott decision was overturned by the 13th and 14th Amendments to the Constitution.

Electrical—using or having to do with electricity; exciting; thrilling.

Electricity—electrical current; a physical phenomenon caused by the movement of certain charged particles such as electrons, especially between points having different electrical charges, and seen in naturally occurring phenomena such as lightning and magnetic attraction and repulsion.

Emancipation Proclamation—the declaration first introduced in 1862 by President Lincoln that freed all the slaves from Confederate states that were not yet under Union control during the United States Civil War.

Emulated—to try to be the same as; to follow the manner or pattern of; attempt to resemble; mimic.
Enslaved--to make a slave of.
Excellent—extremely good; superior; of high quality.
Entiled—to be call by a particular title or name.
Filament—in an electrical device such as a light bulb; a fine wire that lights or heats up when current is passed.
Illumination—the intensity of light per unit of area of a surface exposed to light, a light or lighting.
Incandescent—giving off light as a result of heating; very bright or glowing; showing brilliance or passion. Installation—to make ready for use; the act of installing or condition of being installed.
Magnitude—the measure of brightness; size, extent, or dimension; greatness or importance.
Mastered—to develop skill in or knowledge of something; expertness at.
Mechanical Drawing—descriptive precision drawing, often to scale, that is done with the aid of such implements as T squares, compasses, and French curves; drafting.
Merger—the combining of two or more companies into one, or the transfer of the property of one company to another.
Observing—to watch closely or make a systematic observation of
Patent— a property right that gives an inventor the legal ability to stop others from making, using, or selling an invention for a certain amount of time.
Philanthropist—a person who give their time, talent, or treasure to make a difference in the lives of others.
Practicing—to do over and over; repeated performance in order to become skillful.
Reknown—wide honor and acclaim; fame.
Renaissance man—a man who is knowledgeable, educated, or proficient in a wide range of fields.
Specialization—specific pursuit or field of study.
Surpass—to be better than or exceed in talent, accomplishment, or the like.
Thoroughfare—a street that opens at both ends into other streets.

"Add to this the pride of achievement; a desire to rank among the most successful souls on earth, and we have the factors which have brought some of the ablest of human beings into the limelight that revealed them to an admiring world, as leaders and examples".

www.ingramcontent.com/pod-product-compliance
Lightning Source LLC
Chambersburg PA
CBHW041744040426
42444CB00001B/19